P9-DHN-176

CASTLETON FREE LIBRARY
P.O. BOX 296 MAIN ST.
CASTLETON, VT 05735

WITHDRAWN

EXPLORERS, TRAPPERS, AND GUIDES

EXPLORERS, TRAPPERS, AND GUIDES

JUDITH BENTLEY

TWENTY–FIRST CENTURY BOOKS

A Division of Henry Holt and Company
New York

Twenty-First Century Books
A Division of Henry Holt and Company, Inc.
115 West 18th Street
New York, NY 10011

Henry Holt® and colophon are trademarks of
Henry Holt and Company, Inc.
Publishers since 1866

Text Copyright © 1995 by Judith Bentley
All rights reserved.
Published in Canada by Fitzhenry & Whiteside Ltd.
195 Allstate Parkway
Markham, Ontario L3R 4T8

Library of Congress Cataloging-in-Publication Data
Bentley, Judith.
Explorers, trappers, and guides / Judith Bentley. — 1st ed.
p. cm. — (Settling the west)
Includes bibliographical references (p.) and index.
1. Northwestern States—Discovery and exploration—Juvenile literature. 2.
Northwestern States—History—Juvenile literature. 3. Explorers—Northwestern
States—History—19th century—Juvenile literature. 4. Trappers—West (U.S.)—
History—19th century—Juvenile literature. I. Title. II. Series.
F597.B476 1995
979.5′01—dc20   94–39895
                                                              CIP
                                                              AC

ISBN 0–8050–2995–8
First Edition 1995

Cover design by Kelly Soong
Interior design by Helene Berinsky

Printed in the United States of America
All first editions are printed on acid-free paper ∞.
10 9 8 7 6 5 4 3 2 1

Photo Credits
pp. 2, 12, 16, 29, 32 (both), 40, 42, 43 (inset), 43, 53, 64: North Wind Picture Archives;
pp. 20, 77; The Bettmann Archive; p. 22 (inset): Oregon Historical Society/OrHi 586; p.
22: Oregon Historical Society/OrHi 91188; p. 44: Oregon Historical Society/B. C.
Towne Photo/OrHi 73273; p. 47: Oregon Historical Society/OrHi 19683A; p. 49: Photo
Researchers, Inc. Photograph by Pat and Tom Leeson; p. 56: Photo Researchers, Inc.
Photograph by Lowell Georgia; pp. 61, 75, 78: Nevada Historical Society; p. 67:
Oregon Historical Society/OrHi 35789; p. 71: Photo Researchers, Inc. Photograph by
Jim Steinberg.

EDITOR'S NOTE

A great deal of research went into finding interesting first-person accounts that would give the reader a vivid picture of life on the western frontier. In order to retain the "flavor" of these accounts, original spelling and punctuation have been kept in most instances.

History told in the words of men and women who lived at the time lets us become a part of their lives . . . lives of ordinary people who met extraordinary challenges to settle the West.

—P.C.

ACKNOWLEDGMENTS

For this book, I would like to acknowledge the help of Pat Culleton, senior editor at Twenty-First Century Books, and Laura Phipps and Anne Bentley for research.

—J.B.

CONTENTS

Introduction: First Glimpses   11

1 The Journey   19

2 Encounters Along the Coast   28

3 Exploring the Interior   37

4 The Fur-Trapping Life   51

5 Contact and Conflict   63

6 Guides for the Emigrants   73

Source Notes   82

Further Reading   90

Index   94

SETTLING THE WEST
Many of the places mentioned in the series are located on this map.

MAJOR TRAILS TO THE WEST

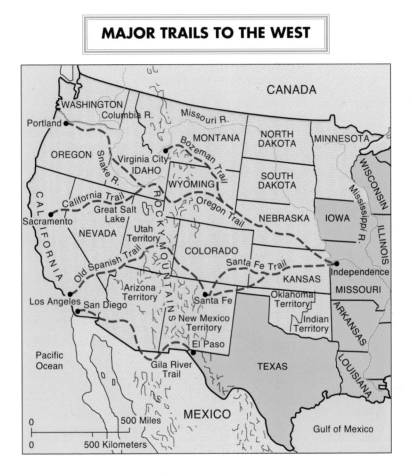

INTRODUCTION: FIRST GLIMPSES

I trust that God will give me the strength to reach San Diego, as He has given me the strength to come so far," wrote Junípero Serra, a Franciscan friar, in 1769.[1] Serra was 8,000 miles from his birthplace, Majorca, but he was walking and riding another 900 miles from Mexico to California.

"For the first time in my life I quitted the place of my birth and was separated from beloved parents and intimate friends," wrote Gabriel Franchere, a young French-Canadian on board an American ship to the Pacific in 1810.[2]

"Well, I am off at last, but who can say when or where I shall stop?" asked William Marshall Anderson, in 1834, leaving Kentucky. "We are finally up and off for the west, the far west. Where is that? I had always believed I had been born in the West; but no, here we go in search of it, farther on, farther on."[3]

In search of the Far West of North America, they came from all over the globe—on foot, on ship, on horseback, or mule.

This statue of Father Junípero Serra stands outside the San Diego Mission in California.

What kind of person would leave home and set off with only a fragment of a map, enough food and water to last perhaps half of the journey, and a 50 percent chance of returning alive?

They were mainly men and boys at first: sailors, captains, soldiers, cooks, ships' boys, carpenters, coopers, hunters, friars like Serra, clerks like Franchere, or just adventurers like Anderson, who was traveling for his health. They were Spanish, Italian, English, Scottish, Russian—and American from the young United States to the East.

Some of the very first may have been Chinese or Japanese, sailing east across the Pacific Ocean in the 1400s. Pieces of Chinese ceramics have been found on the West Coast of the continent, but no written word has been recovered as evidence of their voyage.[4]

As early as 1536, four Spaniards, including a black man named Estevanico, stumbled thousands of miles roughly along the Rio Grande in the direction of the setting sun. They were the only survivors of an expedition sent from Cuba to the west coast of the Florida peninsula.

Shipwrecked and starving, they wandered for eight years and almost reached the Pacific Ocean, crossing parts of the continent never before seen by Europeans.

Looking for a way home along the northern Pacific coast, the English privateer Francis Drake landed in 1577 near present-day San Francisco for repairs to his ship. Fifteen years later, a sailor named Juan de Fuca claimed he had been on a caravel that discovered a broad inlet of sea in colder waters to the north. The land around it, he said, was "very fruitful and rich in gold, silver, and pearls. . . ."[5]

These early tales started wild rumors in the capitals of Europe, Russia, and Mexico. The governor of Mexico met the four survivors from Florida and heard their tales of turquoise, emerald-tipped arrowheads, and coral beads. The English thought the "broad inlet of sea" might be a water passage across the vast North American continent.

The Russians already knew there was wealth to be found in animal furs.

Rumors of wealth and the certain knowledge that unknown lands and peoples existed drew the adventurous. Men like Serra, Franchere, and Anderson, who had so far lived fairly ordinary lives, packed a few belongings and set off.

Father Serra started walking because he was devoted to religion, to converting the peoples of the New World to Catholicism. He set up several missions "for the greater glory of God and the conversion of the pagans to our holy Catholic faith."[6]

With him came soldiers, and they represented those who wanted to claim political possession of the West. "In places where it seems opportune, you will leave some coins buried and in a bottle news of the exploration with the date on which it was carried out," Captain Alejandro Malaspina instructed his Spanish crewmen in 1791, wanting to leave a claim of possession.[7]

Along with religious and political motives were scientific reasons. "You will bear in mind at the same time how important the physical reconnaissance of the coast that we frequent is to us," Malaspina also instructed his crew, "and thus you will not fail to gather specimens of everything belonging to the three kingdoms of natural history. . . ."[8]

For young men like Franchere it was a chance to try their luck. "The desire of seeing strange countries, joined to that of acquiring a fortune" were the reasons he gave for leaving home.[9]

Serra, too, was attracted by the new. "It is not from a want of love that I have not answered some of the letters I have received from Your Reverence," Serra wrote home to his nephew, a friar in Spain. "I could have kept up correspondence with various persons. . . . But if I was to retain forever in memory what I had left behind, what would have been the purpose in leaving it in the first place?"[10]

They came to a land that was already inhabited by people rich in oral tradition, but the land had not been described in written words. High on rocks guarding the Columbia River, in the Valley of Fire in Nevada, and in the "hot-rooms" of the pueblos of New Mexico and Arizona, Native American pictographs and paintings told ancient stories. Suddenly on one rock along the Northern Pacific coast appeared the pictograph of a many-masted ship. With the European and American explorers came written words—the logs of ships, the journals of captains, and the diaries and letters of ordinary folk.

Every day on these journeys, someone wrote down the miles traveled or the latitude and longitude reached, the weather, the food eaten or not eaten, the amount of water left, the animals seen, the native peoples encountered. Coins and bottles left by Malaspina's crew were to be noted in the ship's log "as well as everything that occurs on this trip."[11]

"Most vile, thicke, and stinking fogges" were the first words written by Captain Drake to describe the Pacific Coast.[12]

"Sent the yawl ashore for water," a Russian ship's log recorded on July 20, 1741, in the Aleutian Islands. "The yawl returned with water, and the crew reported having come across a fireplace, human tracks, and a fox on the run."[13]

As they crisscrossed the oceans, the captains and leaders left their names on the landscape: Puget Sound, the

These New Mexico pictographs were carved in basalt, a type of volcanic rock.

Bering Strait, Bodega Bay. Overland trekkers added theirs to rivers and peaks. But the ordinary people who could write also left their mark.

"This day I begin too," Anderson wrote, "to scribble down such incidents, accidents and observations, as may occur, during the horseback journey I am now undertaking."[14]

The journals they kept convey a sense of the importance, the newness, and the wonder of their voyages and journeys. Here, in their own words, are first glimpses of the Far West as travelers approached from the North, the West, the South, and the East.

THE JOURNEY

Estevanico and his three companions walked thousands of miles across the Southwest. A later expedition led by Francisco Vásquez de Coronado rode horses, strange animals the American Indians had never seen. Junípero Serra walked and rode mules the 900 miles to California.

But most of the early explorers came by sea. They departed from Plymouth, England; from Cádiz, Spain; from Boston and New York; and from San Blas on the Mexican coast. All except the Spanish from Mexico had to sail halfway around the world to reach the Far West. Their journeys were as remarkable as their discoveries.

In 1790, an American ship under the command of Captain Robert Gray left from Boston for its second trip around the world. The fifth mate on board was sixteen-year-old John Boit, who described the ship as "fited out for a four years cruize, on a trading voyage to the NW Coast of America, China, etc."[1] For its mission of trading, the *Columbia* carried blue cloth, copper, and iron.

Coronado and his followers rode horses, animals never before seen by Indians, when they explored the Southwest in 1540.

Twenty years later, Gabriel Franchere left New York on the *Tonquin*: "All being ready for our departure, we went on board ship and weighed anchor on the 6th of September, in the morning," he wrote with some misgivings. "For the first time in my life, I found myself under way upon the main sea. . . . I remained for a long time with my eyes fixed in the direction of that land which I no longer saw, and almost despaired of ever seeing again."

The first days were the worst. "The wind having increased, the motion of the vessel made us sea-sick, those of us, I mean, who were for the first time at sea."[2]

Once over his seasickness, Franchere was naturally concerned with the food, or "fare," he could expect for the next seven months: "Our fare consisted of fourteen ounces of hard bread, a pound and a quarter of salt beef or one of pork per day, and half a pint of Souchong tea, with sugar, per man." Pork and beef alternated each day, and there was rice and beans, each once a week, and cornmeal pudding with molasses.

Some days fish was added to the diet. "On the 14th we commenced to take flying fish," he wrote. "The 24th, we saw a great quantity of dolphins. We prepared lines and took two of the latter, which we cooked. The flesh of this fish appeared to me excellent."[3]

Both the *Columbia*, with Boit aboard, and the *Tonquin*, with Franchere, sailed south along the coast of South America headed for Cape Horn at the tip. Boit, too, dipped into the bounty of the air and sea. "Dec. 31: [1790] Fresh gales. Caught 16 Albatross's, with a hook and line from the stern, hook'd them in the bill."

Stopping at the Falkland Islands off the coast of Argentina in January 1791 his crew shot upwards of a thousand ducks and geese and six wild hogs: "The fowl was quite tame when we first arriv'd, but they soon was taught the doctrine of self-preservation."[4]

Despite the fresh meat, some members of the crew became sick, and in April, Boit recorded the death of one source of fresh milk: "Departed this life our dear freind Nancy the Goat having been the Captains companion on a former voyage round the Globe but her spirited disposition for adventure led her to undertake a 2d voyage of Circumnavigation; But the various changes of Climate, and sudden transition from the Polar Colds to the tropical heats of the Torrid Zone, prov'd too much for a constitution naturally delicate, At 5 PM Committed her body to the deep She was lamented by those who got a share of her Milk!!"[5]

Besides the Falklands, the Sandwich Islands (Hawaii) were a favorite spot for loading up on vegetables, bananas, coconuts, watermelons, poultry, and pigs.

From those warm, sunny islands, ships sailed into the colder, stormier waters of the North Pacific as they approached the Northwest coast of the continent. "At 1/2 past seven this Morning we saw the Coast of America bearing NE," wrote David Samwell aboard the English ship *Discovery* in 1778. "This Land is high and craggy and mostly covered with Snow. We saw prostigious [prodigious] large flocks of birds flying about. . . . Having squally Wr [weather] with fogs and frequent Showers of Snow, Hail and Sleet, which made it very dangerous to approach this unknown Coast too near where we knew of no Shelter."[6] The *Discovery*'s captain, James Cook, named the place Cape Foul Weather.

Thirteen years later, the *Columbia* "made land" on the Northwest coast: "This day made the land, on the NW Coast of the American Continent between Nootka . . . and Clioquot . . . for these several days past we had seen whales, Drift Wood, feathers, kelp, etc. All signs of its vicinity . . . snow perceivable on some of the mountains," Boit recorded.[7]

The *Columbia* was the first American ship to explore the Northwest coast. Captain Gray came mainly to trade, but he also discovered the mouth of the rumored Great River of the West, which Captain Cook had missed in the foul weather. Gray was the first to cross the river's formidable bar where it met the ocean's tide, and he named the river after his ship, the *Columbia*.

Captain Robert Gray (inset)
named the river he discovered in
1792 for his ship, the Columbia.

While American and English ships had to sail around South America's Cape Horn, "an object of terror to navigators,"[8] the Spanish could depart from ports on the western coast of Mexico. Even on these shorter voyages, there were problems of bad weather and lack of fresh food and water.

In 1775 a frigate under the command of Bruno de Hezeta had instructions to sail as far north as 65° latitude, to present-day Alaska. The chaplain, Benito de la Sierra, first noted health problems among the livestock on board. By the time they reached California, he wrote that the livestock were dying "for lack of anything to eat or drink."

Hezeta decided to send a smaller boat closer to shore to anchor and find wood, water, and fodder for the livestock. But according to Sierra, "although the rowing was kept up all day long they could not get near the shore. . . . The stock of water was examined, nine empty quarter-casks and ninety-four full ones being found, a small quantity for so long a journey."[9]

Water was not the main problem, however. In the early eighteenth century, it was commonly expected that 50 percent of a ship's crew would not return from a long sea voyage. One of the main reasons was scurvy, a disease that "appears with red spots on the arms and legs especially, which afterwards turn black and then blue; there is an extraordinary weakness, a redness, itching, and rottenness of gums and a looseness of teeth. . . . [The] mouth became stincking [the] gummes so rotten that all the flesh did fall out."[10] Eventually sailors weakened and died. On a Russian land and sea expedition that lasted twenty years, the commander himself, Vitus Bering, died of scurvy.

Scurvy can be prevented easily by eating fresh fruit and vegetables rich in vitamin C, but that was not common knowledge at the time, and they were hard to keep on long sea voyages. Captain Cook served sauerkraut, salted cabbage, and carrot marmalade to his crew, with good results. When they were on shore, he told them to gather wild garlic, nettles, wild peas, celery, or leeks to make soups.

Hezeta seemed to have no knowledge of such remedies, and his crew suffered miserably. "Today two of the men were found to be sickening with scurvy," Sierra reported in May 1775, less than two months out to sea. "God forbid that it should spread!"[11]

On July 23, the chaplain noted a favorable wind and clear sky, but "there were sixteen sick men and on examining the whole crew the surgeons found twelve more showing symptoms of scurvy."[12]

By August 11, the naval officers warned the commandant that "they could hardly muster three men to a watch, and to take in a few reefs in the mainsail they had to call on both watches and even then it took much time, and the same with the foretopsail."[13]

Finally persuaded by his officers' warning, Hezeta decided to abandon his instructions and make for the port of Monterey. Once landed, Sierra wrote, "All the morning was spent ashore setting up a shed covered with sails to protect the sick," but it was too late for some. "In the afternoon when the sick were being taken on shore one died in the launch as soon as the wind struck him."[14]

Sierra listed the toll in his journal. On a voyage that started with 92 men, 36 had scurvy; 14 had other maladies; and 12 had died.

The *Columbia*, too, had men sick with scurvy when it arrived on the Northwest coast in 1791, but the treatment was more successful. They "landed the sick immediately on . . . arrivall and pitch'd a tent for their reception," Boit wrote, "and although there was ten of them in the last stage of the Scurvy, still they soon recover'd, upon smelling the turf, and eating Greens of various Kinds."[15]

Keeping the crew in good health was especially important in foul weather, and the Pacific had its share of storms. Sierra made constant note of the direction and strength of the wind.

June 4, 1775: "The day broke clear, but by nine o'clock the sky had clouded over. . . . After dark the wind blew from the east accompanied by rain squalls, the downpour being very trying to the poorly clad sailors."[16]

A month later, "The Frigate rolled so tremendously that we feared she would lose her topmasts; none of us could obtain a moment's sleep."[17]

In such seas, being driven into shore was also a hazard. "On the 12th when we awoke we were so near the land that we could count the trees, and to get away from it we stood farther out to sea."[18]

On the Malaspina expedition in 1791 and 1792, crew members were recruited from the northern Spanish provinces so they could endure the cold weather of the North Pacific, but still there were hardships. Heading east along the Alaska coast in August 1791, Tomas de Suria recorded unmistakable signs of a storm: "A great number of whales and other fish swimming about, jumping and appearing on the surface."

Then "the wind came up from the southeast so excessively strong that it was necessary to handle the ship with every care, furling the topgallant sails, the mainsail and the foretopsail and remaining only with the topsail and the foresail. The wind kept getting stronger every instant, with rain and a very heavy sea. The swells were tremendous and the darkness terrifying." The storm lasted for six days. "There was not a man who could keep his footing, simply from the violence of the wind. . . . The confusion and shouting on the ship, together with the maledictions [curses] of the sailors . . . augmented the terror to such an extent that it seemed as if all the machinery of the universe were ready to destroy us."[19]

Despite the foul weather, scurvy, and rocky coasts, the marine explorers left their marks on maps and their names on their discoveries—the Strait of Juan de Fuca, Grays Harbor, the Bering Strait, Vancouver Island. Some were disappointed by what they didn't find—gold or silver or an easy waterway across the continent. Others published accounts of what they had found: a broad river leading far into the interior; bays and harbors from California to Puget Sound that would shelter more ships; sea otter furs in abundance; plentiful timber and salmon; and Native Americans willing to trade.

Their voyages complete, most of the early explorers happily went home. Returning to Montreal, Franchere found that his family was surprised he was even alive: "I hastened to the paternal roof, where the family were not less surprised than overjoyed at beholding me . . . certainly it was by the goodness of Providence that I found myself thus safe and sound, in the midst of my relations and friends, at the end of a voyage accompanied by so many perils, and in which so many of my companions had met with an untimely death."[20]

Hezeta's crew returned to San Blas "with the greatest contentment," Sierra noted. "Thanks be to God who brought us safely through so many perils!"[21]

ENCOUNTERS ALONG THE COAST

When the first great sails appeared off the rugged, forested coast of the Pacific Northwest, when the first exhausted Spaniards stumbled across the deserts of the far Southwest, both explorers and natives were astounded by each other.

A clerk aboard a Spanish ship in Alaska saw two tiny canoes race to intercept his vessel. "The first view, when they were near, was one of great astonishment, both for the Indians and for us," he wrote, "for the Indians because they did not cease looking at the ships . . . for us, because such strange and marvelous subjects presented themselves to our sight."[1] What he saw were Tlingit Indians, dressed in skins from what he thought were bears, tigers, lions, deer, and marmots.

A young Indian checking elk pits in northern California looked up and saw approaching "a strange human, followed by an animal never before seen in this region." Swi-net-klas reasoned that it must be a human being. The man had a long beard from his cheeks to his chest, and a round hat of fur; his feet and calves were "covered with skins." He carried "something" in one hand over his shoulder (a rifle), and in his other hand he had strings leading the strange animal (a horse).[2]

A village of Indians on the Cowlitz River in what is now the state of Washington "regarded us with curiosity and astonishment," wrote a clerk on a fur-trading expedition, "lifting the legs of our trowsers and opening our shirts to see if the skin of our bodies resembled that of our faces and hands."[3]

These first encounters between Europeans and Americans and the many coastal and Southwest Indian tribes were marked by curiosity about their differences. When Coronado marched through the Southwest, word

When Indians of the Northwest first saw white trappers, they were astonished at the color of the trappers' skin and at the strange beasts they rode.

passed among the Indian tribes of "very fierce people who rode about on beasts which ate people. . . . This information was generally believed by those who had never seen horses," one of the soldiers wrote, "although it was so strange as to cause much wonder."[4]

Not only horses but guns and gunpowder were entirely new to the natives. When Robert Gray's expedition "met with some Indians that was a little troubelsome . . . by firing a musket over their heads they soon went off."[5]

But there were unexpected similarities, too. "Above 300 of the Natives was along side in the course of the day," John Boit recorded the first day the *Columbia* anchored off shore. "Their canoes was made from the body of a tree, with stem and stern peices, neatly fixd on. Their models was not unlike our Nantucket whale boats. . . . They all appeared very freindly, brought us plenty of fish and Greens."[6]

At first landing on the Northwest coast, Captain James Cook's crew and the natives exchanged songs as a way of getting to know each other. After thirty or forty canoes surrounded the ship, a few stayed at nighttime in a cluster, a small distance from the ship. "As it were to bid us a good night the people in them sang in concert in no disagreeable Stile; this Mark of their Attention to us we were unwiling to pass over unnoticed & therefore gave them in return a few tunes on two french Horns . . . to these they were very attentive. . . . [After] another Song from the Indians . . . we gave them a Tune on the Drum & Fife to which they paid the same attention as they had done to the Horns. These Canoes staid by the Ship most part of the Night seemingly with no other View but that of gratifying their curiosity."[7]

The Spanish called the people they encountered Indians because Columbus thought he had landed in India. The misnomer has lasted for centuries. To the Russians on Bering's ships, the first people they met in North America were simply the "Americans." "When we had accepted the presents the Americans pulled away for the shore," wrote Safron Khitrov in the ship's log.[8]

These Americans, in fact, had some Asian features and may have crossed over a land bridge between Siberia and Alaska thousands of years ago, then slowly migrated south. Wherever they came from, they had been in the West a long time.

Francisco Vásquez de Coronado was searching for cities of gold in the Southwest when he found, instead, what is now the longest continually inhabited settlement in the United States, the pueblo of Acoma. The Acoma people had been living there for 500 years when Coronado arrived in 1540, and they have remained to this day. There was a good reason for the community's endurance. "The village was very strong because it was up on a rock out of reach," wrote the soldier Pedro de Castaneda, "having steep sides in every direction, and so high that it was a very good musket that could throw a ball as high."[9]

When newcomers and natives met, appearance was usually the first item of curiosity. Indian tribes and nations varied greatly in dress, from complete nudity to elaborate clothing of furs, cedar bark, blankets made from dogs' hair, and cloth and feather robes.

Among the Queen Charlotte Islands, off the coast of what is now British Columbia, Boit noted an unusual custom of decoration. "The Men go quite naked, except a skin over the shoulder. the Women are entirely cover'd with garments of their own manufactory, from the bark of Tree [cedar bark]. They appear to carry full sway over the men and have an incision cut through the under lip, which they spread out with a piece of wood about the size and shape of a Goose egg [some much larger]. It's considered as an ornament, but in my opinion looks very gastly. Some of them booms out two inches from the chin."[10]

These sections of a mural shows how Kiva Indians of New Mexico dressed around 1500.

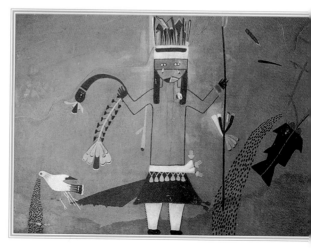

By contrast, the Indians of the Southwest covered their bodies, Castañeda wrote, "with cloths made like a sort of table napkin, with fringed edges and a tassel at each corner, which they tie over the hips. They wear long robes of feathers and of the skins of hares, and cotton blankets."[11]

Once past appearances, each side was eager to trade. Junípero Serra's expedition was followed by Indians who wanted the Spaniards' clothes, boots, leather jackets, and even the priest's clothing, or habit. Serra's glasses were passed around once, and a man ran off with them. "God knows what it cost me to recover them," he wrote.[12]

"The anxiousness with which our people bought the vilest objects for the sole reason of it having belonged to the natives, opened every minute a new line of trade," commented Tomas de Suria far to the north among the Tlingit.[13] Soon a set price was established of one three-centimeter nail for a salmon. Farther south along the coast at Nootka, the Indians wanted copper and abalone shells, which the Spanish could bring from Monterey, California.

What the newcomers most wanted to trade for was sea otter skins. Captain Cook started the trade when his men loaded up on furs as they headed for the North Pole. "Early this Morning we were surrounded by a great Number of Canoes full of People, who brought with them the Fur of the Sea Beaver & Bear skins with which they were cloathed to sell," wrote David Samwell at Nootka Sound in 1778. "These to us who were bound for the North Pole were valuable articles and every one endeavoured to supply himself with some of them, but having been so lavish of our Spike nails & Hatchets among the beautiful Girls of the South Sea Islands we had but few of these Articles left to purchase them with." They discovered that wire hoops, buttons, and pieces of cloth or brass would do: "We stripped our Cloaths for them and knocked our Pans and Teakettles to pieces."[14]

When Cook's ships eventually arrived in Canton, China, the sailors found they had made an excellent bargain, for the furs they had used to keep themselves warm brought high prices at resale. Word reached Europe and the United States of the "soft gold" to be found in the Northwest.

Just four years later, John Boit's journal from the *Columbia* is full of such exchanges: "We purchas'd many of the Sea Otter skins in exchange for Copper and blue Cloth."[15]

"We purchased a Good Lot of furs, cheifly for Iron and Cloth."[16]

"During our short stay [near the mouth of the Columbia River] we collected 150 otter, 300 Beaver, and twice the Number of other land furs."[17]

Besides fur, the coastal Indians provided food, particularly salmon, the main element of their diet. Lieutenant Salamanca, on Malaspina's expedition, describes a salmon feast to which he was invited by the Nootka chief, Maquinna. "One day when we went to Maquinnas' house, he had a banquet in our honour. . . . They put down new mats for us to sit on. They gave us a salmon which were still scarce (it is of the previous year and they conserve it with continuous smoke without salt or any other assistance). . . . His people roasted it over the coals with great cleanliness so it would not be repugnant to us. . . . He showed us several pieces of whale meat which he did not serve, giving us to understand by signs that it would turn our stomachs."[18]

Explorers also learned how the Native Americans

used the materials at hand to fashion what they needed. The Northwest coast had plentiful supplies of timber, which Suria knew would be useful for masts and planking. He also noted "a type of short grass that is found in these high latitudes which they call moss. It grows in the shade and on the rocks." The Indians wove with the moss, but he thought it could also be used to caulk ships. "After it is dry, it is placed between various boards and once it enters the water it expands so as to make it as tight as if done with oakum and of greater duration."[19]

These first encounters established lasting patterns of interaction between Native Americans and European Americans. In California, the Spanish converted the Indians to Christianity and put them to work farming. On the Northwest coast, both sides benefited from trade: food and furs for nails, cloth, abalone shells, and beads. But when traders took unfair advantage of the native peoples or insulted their hosts or when Indians stole items they wanted, friendliness could change to hostility. A violent act by one side often led to revenge by the other.

John Boit was called on to perform an act he found quite distasteful. Indians had attacked one of Gray's ships in an attempt to capture it. In retaliation, Gray ordered the burning of a village.

"I am sorry to be under the nessescity of remarking that this day I was sent with three boats, all well man'd and arm'd, to destroy the Village of Opitsatah it was a Command I was no ways tenacious off, and am greived to think Capt. Gray shou'd let his passions go so far."[20]

It was not only the act of burning but the culture destroyed that bothered Boit. The village had about 200 houses, he wrote, "generally well built for Indians ev'ry door that you enter'd was in resemblance to an human and Beasts head, the passage being through the mouth, besides which there was much more rude carved work about the dwellings some of which was by no means innelegant. This fine Village, the Work of Ages, was in a short time totally destroy'd."[21]

A quieter form of violence was disease. Sailors who had sexual relations with Indian women passed on venereal disease, despite the efforts of some captains to prevent its spread. Smallpox, common in the eighteenth and nineteenth centuries, was especially deadly to natives who had developed no immunity to it.

"Twas evident that these Natives had been visited by that scourge of mankind the Smallpox," Suria observed at a village on the Strait of Juan de Fuca. "The Spaniards as the natives say brought it among them."[22]

Bringing iron, guns, and disease and taking furs, maps, and specimens, the explorers sailed away. They left signs of their visits: Spanish coins appeared in Indian jewelry; a red-haired child was born in the Clatsop tribe; the name Mount Rainier replaced Tahoma. In the journals they published, too, were descriptions of the "Americans" they had found, a native people both fascinating and troubling to those who later wanted to live where they lived.

3

EXPLORING
THE INTERIOR

"Alexander Mackenzie, from Canada, by land, the twenty-second of July, one thousand seven hundred and ninety-three," wrote the Scottish explorer, using a mixture of vermilion and melted grease to paint his name on a rock near the British Columbia coast.[1]

"William Clark December 3rd 1805. By Land from the U. States in 1804 and 1805," carved the American explorer on a tall yellow pine overlooking the Pacific Ocean near the Columbia River.[2]

This early-day graffiti was not just a boast but a claim. Both men were crossing the North American continent from two different countries. British fur trading companies sent men like Alexander Mackenzie down rivers and lakes from the Canadian north, looking for a water route to carry furs to the Pacific. United States president Thomas Jefferson sent William Clark and Meriwether Lewis overland to survey the territory the United States had just bought from France. Even in this vast western wilderness, British and

American paths crossed as both countries explored the interior.

Lewis and Clark had instructions to ascend the Missouri River to its source, cross the Rocky Mountains, and find the best waterway connection to the Pacific. For their mission, they recruited "some good hunters, stout healthy unmarried young men, accustomed to the woods, and capable of bearing bodily fatigue to a pretty considerable extent."[3]

A "rough and burly frontiersman" named Patrick Gass joined this expedition called the Corps of Discovery, with some misgivings. "The best authenticated accounts informed us," Gass wrote at the beginning, "that we were to pass through a country possessed by numerous, powerful and warlike nations of savages, of gigantic stature, fierce, treacherous and cruel; and particularly hostile to white men."[4]

The first nation encountered was hardly warlike or savage. After traveling a short distance up the Missouri, the corps wintered with the friendly Mandan people, then pushed off in earnest in the spring of 1805. Next they met the Sioux. Sixty Sioux encamped on the opposite shore of the Missouri River, Gass wrote, "and some corn and tobacco were sent over to them. . . . They killed a dog as a token of friendship. One of our men killed a deer."

The next morning, four of the Sioux who were musicians came over the river and "went backwards and forwards, through and round our camp, singing and making a noise. After that ceremony was over they all sat in Council." An evening of talking, gifts, music, and dancing followed, and the two groups parted company the next morning on friendly terms.

For food on the journey, the corps caught fish and hunted deer. "We are generally well supplied with catfish, the best I have ever seen," Gass wrote one day. On another, "Captain Clarke and ten of the party went to the Maha creek to fish, and caught 387 fish of different kinds." They also killed pelicans whose pouches could be used to carry five gallons of water each.

They were not so successful with a bear they encountered. "In the evening we killed a large bear in the river; but he sunk and we did not get him."

Likewise the hunters killed a buffalo but could not bring the carcass back to camp before nightfall. One of the men left his hat, hoping the human smell would ward off the wolves, but the next morning "when we came to the place, we found the wolves had devoured the carcase and carried off the hat."[5]

Following the Missouri far to the north, then up the Jefferson River into Montana's Bitterroot Valley, the corps abandoned their boats and approached the Rocky Mountains through a wild and desolate country. "In the Alps, civilization extends right up to the fringe of the eternal ice," wrote a German mapmaker on a later expedition. "Here everything is wild, almost sterile for thousands of miles."[6]

Almost through the mountains by September 1805, the corps longed for more food and level ground. "The men are becoming lean and debilitated, on account of the scarcity and poor quality of the provision on which we subsist," Gass lamented. When a valley appeared forty miles ahead, however, "there was as much joy and rejoicing among the corps, as happens among passengers at sea, who have experienced a dangerous and protracted voyage, when they first discover land on the long looked for coast."[7]

Once out of the Rockies, they built new boats to travel down the Clearwater and Columbia Rivers, finally reaching the Pacific coast. There, with the ocean roaring "like a repeeted roling thunder," Clark carved his name and date on a pine tree.[8] The corps built huts to protect themselves from the rain, made salt from the seawater, and preserved meat for the winter. On Christmas Day they moved in, and "at day break all the men paraded and fired a round of small arms, wishing the Commanding Officers a merry Christmas."[9]

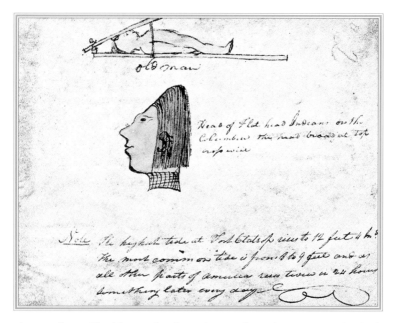

A page from Clark's notebook, written when the Lewis and Clark expedition traveled down the Columbia River.

Having reached their goal, the corps returned to the United States by more southern routes. Arriving in St. Louis in late September of 1806, Lewis and Clark sat down to write letters to the president and reports of their discoveries. They described a continent far wider than previously thought and rich in natural resources like fur.

Although Mackenzie had reached the Pacific coast, he had not found a navigable east-west waterway. So a few years after the Lewis and Clark expedition, the North West Company, a British fur-trading company, sent David Thompson to map the Columbia River. Thompson spent five years on the river, covering the entire length from its source in Canada to its mouth on the Pacific Ocean. Paddling the canoes were the voyageurs, men employed by fur companies to transport goods and supplies to and from the remote fur-trading posts. These French-Canadians were known for their river-running skills.

"No men in the world are more severely worked than these Canadian voyageurs," wrote a young British officer. Each canoe could carry five tons of provisions with a crew of ten. At portages, six men carried the canoe, which could weigh about 1,500 pounds. The rest carried the cargo, in packs of 90 pounds, "each man bearing two packs, and sometimes, as a display of strength, three. . . . They smoke almost incessantly, and sing peculiar songs, which are the same their fathers and grandfathers and probably their great-grandfathers sang before them."[10]

When Thompson and his voyageurs arrived at the mouth of the Columbia in July 1812, he found an American fur-trading post already established there. The businessman John Jacob Astor had sent two expeditions, one by land and one by sea, to enter the fur trade. The sea expedition arrived in the fall of 1811, cut down some of the plentiful trees, and built a trading post named Astoria.

Although their motive was profit, fur traders like the Astorians had to be explorers, too. There were no wagon tracks to follow or road maps of the country they crossed, only the advice of Indians or the few reports of previous journeys.

The overland Astoria expedition had started off well

When a river became impassible, the crew had to carry everything overland until they could get back on the river.

An expedition sent by John Jacob Astor (inset) established the trading post Astoria in 1811 on the Columbia River.

enough, following Lewis and Clark's northern route, but they left the Missouri River to follow the Platte River instead, then passed around the northern end of the mountains of the Wind River Range through Union Pass. The route proved more difficult.

On the day before Christmas, 1811, Wilson Price Hunt, the leader, recorded: "My party now consisted of thirty-two whites, a woman more than eight months pregnant [the Indian wife of the Sioux interpreter], her two children, and three Indians. We had only five wretched horses for our food during the passage of the mountains."[11]

Then they made a serious mistake, trying to follow the Snake River to reach the Columbia. A later traveler confirmed how impassible the Snake was: "This Snake River is interesting, I must confess, no matter how awful the country around it may be. The most beautiful little waterfalls, twenty to forty feet high. Then steep, volcanic, rocky shores along which one can travel for days without being able to find a place to get down to the stream. This and the lack of grass makes traveling very difficult."[12]

Part of Hunt's group finally reached the Columbia, but the newborn baby had died. "We had travelled 1751 miles, we had endured all the hardships imaginable," Hunt wrote. "With difficulty I expressed the joy at sight of this river."[13] Stragglers stumbled into Astoria, exhausted and near starvation, in January and February 1812.

A view of the treacherous Snake River

Life at Astoria soon settled into a routine. The young clerk Gabriel Franchere had arrived with the sea expedition. After a New Year's celebration, he reported, "our people resumed their ordinary occupations: while some cut timber for building, and others made charcoal for the blacksmith, the carpenter constructed a barge, and the cooper made barels for the use of the posts we proposed to establish in the interior."[14]

When members of Hunt's overland expedition had recovered, trading parties were sent out, leaving only Franchere and one other clerk at the fort. Luckily a supply ship, the *Beaver*, had brought a load of books. "In the intervals of our daily duties, we amused ourselves with music and reading; having some instruments and a choice library. Otherwise we should have passed our time in a state of insufferable ennui, at this rainy season, in the midst of the deep mud which surrounded us."[15]

As Franchere settled in with his books, an eighteen-year-old Irish clerk, Ross Cox, headed up the Columbia River with a trading party. They left in bateaux—small flat-bottomed boats—and light wooden canoes, knowing the Columbia River was not completely navigable. For the first 170 miles the ride was smooth until they reached a point where the Columbia narrows. Thereafter "a succession of boiling whirlpools" characterized the river at the point known as The Dalles. "Above this channel for four or five miles the river is one deep rapid. . . . For upwards of half a mile, the immense waters of the Columbia are one mass of foam."[16] Cox's party hefted their loads around the rapids for nearly nine miles.

On shore, too, there were dangers as the party reached dry, hot regions. Cox described an encounter between a rattlesnake and a man named La Course: "This man had stretched himself on the ground, after the fatigue of the day, with his head resting on a small package of goods, and quickly fell asleep. While in this situation I passed him, and was almost petrified at seeing a large rattlesnake moving from his side to his left breast.

"My first impulse was to alarm La Course; but an old Canadian whom I beckoned to the spot requested me to make no noise, alleging it would merely cross the body and go away."[17] It didn't, stopping to coil itself on the man's left shoulder.

Two men approached the snake in front to divert it while another came from behind with a long stick. As the men moved, the snake "instantly raised its head, darted out its forked tongue, and shook its rattles; all indications of anger. Everyone was now in a state of feverish agitation as to the fate of poor La Course, who still lay slumbering, unconscious of his danger." The man with the stick "suddenly placed one end of it under the coiled reptile and succeeded in pitching it upwards of ten feet from the man's body.

"A shout of joy was the first intimation to La Course of his wonderful escape." The man with the stick killed the snake, which the Canadians found quite tasty. Searching under rocks, the party found upwards of fifty more rattlesnakes, "all of which we destroyed. . . ."[18]

As they sought new tribes to trade with and possible sites for trading posts, groups like Cox's were also adding to the geographical knowledge of the Far West. An Astorian, Robert Stuart, followed an Indian trail on the way back east and "discovered" South Pass, a pass through the Rocky Mountains that later became the main gateway of the Oregon Trail.

Not all exploring, however, was for the purposes of trapping or trading. In the 1820s, a Scottish botanist, David Douglas, documented plant and animal life around the Columbia River for the Hudson's Bay Company. Despite the annoyances and dangers, Douglas clearly relished the outdoor life. "In England," he wrote, "people shudder at the idea of sleeping with a window open; here, each individual takes his blanket and with all the complacency of

David Douglas was a Scottish botanist who doc-
umented plant and animal life on the Columbia
River in the 1820s.

mind that can be imagined throws himself on the sand or under a bush just as if he were going to bed."[19]

Douglas brought some European habits, too. His Indian canoe men and guides thought him a funny sight for drinking boiling water (tea), "lighting my tobacco pipe with my lens and the sun. . . . But above all, to place a pair of spectacles on the nose is beyond all their comprehension! They immediately place the hand tight on the mouth, a gesture of dread or astonishment."[20]

After a year of collecting, Douglas sent back to the Horticultural Society of London "three bundles of dry plants (ninety-seven distinct species), forty-five papers of seeds, three Arctomys [marmots], and one curious rat, which I hope you will receive safe." He also sent measurements of a species of remarkable pine trees. "The largest one I could find that was blown down by the wind," he recorded, was 57 feet, 9 inches in circumference, 3 feet from the ground, and 215 feet long, or two-thirds of a football field tall.[21]

Such descriptions of mammoth trees eventually brought loggers to the Far West, but at the time Douglas had the wilderness almost to himself. When he received letters from England delivered by the Hudson's Bay Company's annual ship to Fort Vancouver, "I am not ashamed to say that (although it might be thought weakness by some) I rose from my mat four different times during the night to read my letters; in fact before morning I might say I had them by heart—my eyes never closed."[22]

Although Douglas followed his scientific curiosity, young men like Franchere and Cox had left the comforts of home hoping to make their fortunes. Those dreams ended when the War of 1812 broke out between the United States

The Douglas fir, named for David Douglas, is the source of more lumber than any other kind of tree in North America. A Douglas fir may grow up to 250 feet tall and live up to 800 years.

and Great Britain. With rumors abounding that a British man-of-war would soon seize Astoria, the men at the post sold it to a British fur company, the North West Company.

"It was thus, that after having passed the seas, and suffered all sorts of fatigues and privations, I lost in a moment all my hopes of fortune," Franchere despaired.[23] He decided to go home.

Cox, too, tired of "the Indian country. Horse-racing, deer-hunting and grouse-shooting were pleasant pastimes enough," he noted, "but the want of companionable society rendered every amusement 'stale, flat, and unprofitable.'"[24] After a dreary five months alone at Fort Okanagon, a fur company post, he returned to Montreal in September 1817.

As the Astorians headed home, the maritime fur trade came to a close. The sea otters had almost vanished, their shimmering fur too tempting a target. While crisscrossing the continent, however, these inland explorers had recorded passes through the mountains, traced the routes of long rivers, and discovered a new "soft gold"—the fur of the beaver. In journals and published accounts, they passed on advice to a new wave of travelers who would add their own discoveries to the developing map of the West.

4

THE FUR-TRAPPING LIFE

Needed: "100 young men to ascend the Mo. [Missouri River] to its source, there to be employed for one, two, or three years," read an ad in a Missouri newspaper in 1822.[1]

The advertiser wanted fur trappers. During the 1820s and 1830s, nearly 1,000 mountain men headed into the valleys and streams of the Rocky Mountains to trap beaver. Beaver hats and fur-trimmed gowns and bonnets were high fashion in New York, Boston, and London.

James Clyman was one of the thousand. A surveyor who also read Shakespeare and wrote short poems, Clyman had come to St. Louis to be paid for the surveying work he had done in Illinois. While there, he sought out the man who had placed the ad.

"I heard a report that general William H Ashly was engageing men for a Trip to the mouth of the Yellow Stone river," Clyman wrote. Ashley gave him "a lenthy acount of game found in that Region Deer, elk, Bear and Buffalo but to crown all immence Quantities of Beaver whose skins ware verry valuable selling for $5 to $8 a pound at that time in St. Louis and the men he wished to engage were to [be] huters trappers and traders for furs and peltrees."[2]

Since good spelling was not a qualification for the job, Clyman signed on and bought some new clothes for the trip.

"I think I was something of a fop in those days and sometimes have a good laugh to think how I must have looked in my fringed suit of buckskin with ruffled shirt to match."[3]

Soon, however, he looked and smelled like the rest: "A suit of clothes is seldom washed or turned from the time it is first worn until it is laid aside," wrote a fellow traveler. "Caps and hats are made of beaver and otter skins, the skins of buffalo calves, &c. Some of these are fantastically ornamented with tails and horns." Fringes "are six or seven inches long, and hung densely on every seam . . . of the hunting shirt and leggins. Indeed their weight is a great burden."[4]

Overcoats made from blankets were added for warmth in the mountains. Mountaineers also carried "possible sacks," sacks containing everything a trapper could possibly need in the mountains.

In search of pelts, such parties as Ashley's followed the Missouri, the Platte, the Kansas, the Yellowstone, the Green, the Colorado, the Bear, and the Arkansas Rivers. They looked for the well-known signs of beaver, such as the quantity of wood cut on a river's banks.

To catch the animals, traps would be placed at strategic locations along the beaver's daily route, at the base of its slides into the water or near the paths it dragged wood along. In his possible sack, each trapper also kept cas-

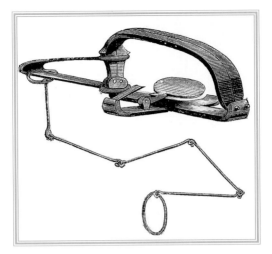

This early trap was used to catch muskrat.
A beaver trap is very similar.

toreum—a mixture made from the beaver's own secretion, castor, and assorted spices such as nutmeg, cloves, and cinnamon. Despite the added scents, the trappers usually smelled like the beaver castor they carried.

The trapper would set the trap, dip a twig in the castoreum, and place it in the trap so the beaver would have to step in it to sniff the twig. Once caught in the trap, the beaver usually drowned. Then it was skinned on the spot, the pelt roughly cured by scraping it free of meat and stretching it to dry on a willow frame. The trapper took only the pelt, the castoreum gland, and the tail for eating.

Ashley's expedition found plenty of beaver, which made him a rich man. James Clyman stayed in the mountains for four years and brought back 278 pounds of beaver. He sold the furs for $1,251 and spent the money on farmland.

Besides the challenge of trapping enough beaver to pay their costs, trappers faced the obstacles and excitement of new terrain. In pursuit of beaver, they crossed faster rivers, deeper canyons, higher mountains, and drier deserts than they had ever seen before. They depended on canoes, horses, mules, and their feet but sometimes learned from the Indian tribes that had long ago adapted to the differing terrain.

Catherine, whose last name is unknown, was the daughter of a Nez Perce woman and a father who was half Mohawk and half French. She and several women and children joined a fur-trapping expedition with her father and a hundred white men to the Green River country of northern Colorado in 1841. "We left Pierre's hole [in Idaho] . . . when the antelope were fawning in the last month of spring and the first of summer," she recounted to her children.

The women and children on the trip looked out for themselves. "The first river we crossed was a swift stream of about 70 paces broad. The men made rafts to carry their little baggage. The women stripped and lightening their saddles on their best horses plunged into the stream with them, having tied their children one by one on their backs, and swimming along with their horses on the side made several trips that way across the river before they had their children all landed safely, as they would not trust their little ones to the ripples.

"I swam bearing my little brother, whilst my stepmother swam with her young child, my sister. The women were stripped to the cotton shirt. The water was very cold, rushing from its parent springs and higher peaks."[5]

Harrison Rogers described a less successful crossing of the Rogue River in 1828: "All hands up early, some

54

fixing the rafts for crossing the river and others sent after the horses. We had all our goods crossed by 9 o.c. A.M., and then proceeded to drive in the horses; there was 12 drowned in crossing, and I know not the reason without it was driving them in too much crowded one upon another. We have lossed 23 horses and mules within 3 days past."[6]

Solid ground was not without its hazards either, especially ground that came in waves. The tallest obstacles, of course, were the Rocky Mountains. "These are emphatically Rocky mountains, accurately so named," wrote William Anderson in 1834. "Enormous piles of various colored granite, now dark and dull, now grey and sparkling."[7]

The early explorers had discovered ways across the Rockies, but Union Pass was closed by snow when a party led by Jedediah Smith approached in the winter of 1824. Returning to the Crow villages where they had camped, the trappers spread a deerskin on the ground. Using piles of sand to represent the mountain ranges, they asked the Crows how they could get over them to the Green River Valley, which was said to be rich in beaver. The Crows told them about the same pass Robert Stuart had "discovered" in 1812, South Pass. Smith didn't realize the broad low ridge was a pass until he saw waters flowing west instead of east.

Many others who followed recorded the moment they first crossed this Continental Divide. "This evening, with the sun, we passed from the Eastern to Western America . . .," wrote William Anderson. "Yesterday, from a scarecely perceptible elevation, we could distinctly see waters flowing east and west, which enter far, far away into the two rival oceans of this continent."[8]

Beyond the Rockies was the Great Salt Lake, an item

It is easy to see from this photograph why the Rockies were hard to cross in winter.

of great curiosity. "So close to the Salt Lake and we have to get along without salt! Isn't that funny?" wrote Charles Preuss on an expedition in 1843, led by John C. Frémont. Four days later they had arrived: "We found plenty of salt and have boiled down some of it. I believe that three, or certainly four, pounds of water make one pound of salt. I have never seen anything like it. We found the salt fifteen feet deep near the island."[9]

Beyond salty water was dry, arid land, hardly beaver territory, but Jedediah Smith was determined to cross the desert, in 1826, to reach more promising land beyond it. "We frequently travelled without water sometimes for two days over sandy deserts, where there was no sign of vegetation," Smith recorded. Nevertheless, he continued on across the Mojave Desert and the Sierra Nevada, thus completing a new central overland route all the way to the Pacific.

As Smith returned the next year with furs his party had trapped, water again was scarce. Near the present Nevada–Utah border, a member of the expedition gave out completely and had to be left behind. "We could do no good by remaining to die with him," Smith wrote, "and we were not able to help him along, but we left him with feelings only known to those who have been in the same situation and with the hope that we might get relief and return to save his life."[10]

In fact they did. After a few miles of travel they reached a fine stream of water, filled a kettle with several quarts, and hurried back to help the man who was far gone and scarcely able to speak. With water to revive him, he was soon able to travel again, with help, to a spring where they camped. Travelers suffering from thirst were often buried to the neck in sand to prevent further dehydration while water was sought.

Even when found, water could be deceptive. Traveling in 1846, Clyman was in a party that came across pools of water, some with beautiful clear water boiling in them and others emitting quantities of mud. "Into one of these muddy pools my little water spaniel Lucky went," Clyman noted, "poor fellow not knowing that it was Boiling hot he deliberately walked in to the caldron to slake his thirst and cool his limbs when to his sad disappointment and my sorrow he scalded himself allmost instantly to death I felt more for his loss than any other animal I ever lost in my life as he had been my constant companion in all my wandering since I Left Milwawkee."[11]

Dogs, horses, and mules were the companions, feet, and pack carriers for the mountain men. While horses and mules carried food for the humans, trapping parties constantly searched for grass as food for the animals. When grass couldn't be found, the sweet bark of cottonwood trees would do.

For human food, fur-trapping parties carried jerky, which was the dried meat of buffalo, or pemmican, which the Indians made out of dried ground meat, fat, and herbs. These dried foods were for lean times. Usually mountain men preferred fresh game. There were few trimmings. Kit Carson recalled that during his sixteen years in the mountains he had no other food "than that which I could procure with my rifle. Perhaps, once a year, I would have a meal consisting of bread, meat, sugar, and coffee; would consider it a luxury."[12]

In the worst of times, the horses themselves became the food. Killing a horse that was already near starvation could sustain an expedition for a few more days until game was found. "I ate some of it yesterday for the first time," Charles Preuss admitted. "I really cannot say whether it tasted good or bad."[13]

Even with ample food and water, the mountain life was not exactly comfortable. Clyman describes camping "amidtst innumerable swarms of fine large Brown grasshoppers" who were so voracious they had to be beaten off the baggage with sticks.[14]

Two weeks later it was a plague of mosquitoes, for which Clyman had his own spelling. "Toward sundown the Mokotoes made a general and simultanious attact on ourselves and animals and although I had fought mosketois through the wabash Illinois and Mississippi vallies yet I never met with such a Quantity of Blood thirsty animals in any country as we found here your mouth nose Ears Eyse and every other assailable point had its thousand Enemies striving which should be formost in their thirst for Blood."[15]

Despite the hardships, there were also benefits to the mountain life. Climbing "a very lofty and steep Mountain," Anderson exclaimed, "How bright and balmy was the air! how distant and how rugged the view! . . . Here, a solitary eagle, circling in the air. . . . Far far down chrystal streams glisten in the distance. . . . No living thing that touched the earth above me, & Nothing that breathed, between me and the heavens, save the lone eagle, which sprang from the spot on which I stood."[16]

The songs of birds also refreshed several travelers. On the trapping expedition, Catherine saw a beautiful little bird who "had eight different songs of his own and I listened and listened and looked at him again and again, and

I thought of how happy he was at home enjoying his fate whilst we were ranging the waste and wilderness day and night in eagerness and blood, anxious to be rich."[17]

Since trappers spent months alone or with the same few people, the social highlight of the year was the rendezvous. Mountain men, Indians, and traders came together to pick up supplies and trade the furs they had trapped. At the 1834 rendezvous on Hams Fork of the Green River, there were 1,500 people, "a motley set, Whites, French, Yankees, Nes Perces, Flatheads, and Snakes, or Shoshones." The famous hunter Kit Carson was there, as were William Anderson and John K. Townsend writing in their journals.

"Whooping and howling, and quarrelling . . . added to the mounted Indians, who are constantly dashing into and through our camp, yelling like fiends, the barking and baying of savage wolf-dogs, and the incessant cracking of rifles and carbines, render our camp a perfect bedlam," wrote Townsend.[18] Someone chased a bull buffalo through camp just because he said he would. Next came a large grizzly bear that had been frightened from the hills by two boys.

Anderson also noted the Indian women who "are very fine riders, mounting and dismounting with the ease and grace of a cavalier."[19]

Carson recorded that some business was transacted, too. "We disposed of our beaver to procure supplies. Coffee and suger [were] two dollars a pint, powder the same, lead one dollar a bar, and common blankets from fifteen to twenty five dollars apiece."[20]

The rendezvous lifted the spirits of those who had been away from civilization. News from "the United States," of new and old fur grounds, of the appearance and

Kit Carson

disappearance of fur trappers was exchanged. Returning east, William Anderson made another connection with civilized life at Fort William: "August 21, 1834—I have found at this place a long lost (it seems long) friend—the day of the week—This is thursday—Eh bien—I'll hold on to you, henceforth—."[21]

In fact, the days and years of mountain life were running out. These rowdy men and fine horsewomen had one more rendezvous, in 1835. Like the sea otter before them, the beaver, too, were nearly trapped to death. Then large numbers of people began pouring into the Far West, trampling the faint traces across mountains and deserts. Many of the mountain men adapted to the change, becoming guides and hunters for the newcomers, even settling down to farm. For the Native Americans, however, the influx of settlers exacted a much more radical change of life.

CONTACT AND CONFLICT

After the first contacts between newcomers and natives on the Pacific Coast, astonishment and curiosity settled into routine trading. As Americans came up the Missouri River in the early 1800s, however, the Indians of the interior must have watched uneasily. They were eager to trade, yet they didn't want to lose control of the rivers, the buffalo, and the trading relationships they already had with other tribes.

Lewis and Clark had expected to find "numerous, powerful and warlike nations." A few tribes were powerful and warlike, but others were weak or friendly. Like the coastal explorers before them, the overland explorers and trappers found the Native Americans as varied as the terrain that had shaped them.

The first tribes up the Missouri River were the Mandans, who were prosperous and friendly. The next tribe, the Sioux, were haughty and belligerent. They were also a mobile people, using dogs to haul their lodges "made of dressed buffaloe and elk skins."

A Sioux camp on the Mississippi River

"While I was at the Indian camp yesterday," Patrick Gass wrote in his journal, "they yoked a dog to a kind of car, which they have to haul their baggage from one camp to another; the nation having no settled place or village, but are always moving about. The dogs are not large, much resemble a wolf, and will haul about 70 pounds each." He also saw evidence that confirmed the Sioux's warlike reputation: "About 15 days ago they had a battle with the Mahas, of whom they killed 75 men and took 25 women prisoners, whom they have now with them."[1]

Among the Plains Indians were many skilled horsemen, riding the descendants of mustangs Coronado brought to the Plains in the 1540s. "These Indians are the most active horsemen I ever saw," Gass commented on his way back east in May 1806. "They will gallop their horses over precipices, that I should not think of riding over at all."[2]

Another time he noted that, "As we came along today we passed a place where the Indians had driven above an hundred head of buffaloe down a precipice and killed them."[3]

Although Lewis and Clark's encounter with the Sioux was peaceful, the tribe was dominant on the Plains and increasing in size and power. They controlled the upper Missouri River, and fur-trapping expeditions had to talk or bargain or fight their way past them.

Another threatening tribe was the Blackfeet, the only tribe with which the Lewis and Clark expedition fought. The Blackfeet continued to fight the fur trappers who followed that expedition and also fought their own Indian neighbors. Returning from rendezvous in 1834 with a hunting party of fifty men, Kit Carson related that the tribe stymied their trapping efforts that fall. "We started for the country of the Blackfeet Indians, on the head waters of the Missouri. We made a very poor hunt as the Indians were very bad. We had five men killed. A trapper could hardly go a mile without being fired upon. We found that we could do but little in their country, so we started for winter quarters."[4]

Farther to the west were much poorer tribes, including the Shoshones. "They are the poorest and most miserable nation I ever beheld," Gass wrote, "having scarcely any thing to subsist on, except berries and a few fish, which they contrive by some means, to take. . . . They move about in any direction where the berries are most plenty."[5]

The Canadian fur trader Peter Skene Ogden was also dismayed by their poverty: "I had often heard these wretches subsisted on ants, locusts and small fish, in size not larger than minnies [minnows], and I was determined to find out if it was not an exaggeration of late travelers, but to my surprise I found it was the case, for one of their dishes, not of a small size, was filled with ants and on inquiring in what manner they collected them: 'In the morning early before the thaw commences.' The locusts they collect in summer and store up for the winter."

Ogden said they preferred the taste of the ants to that of the grasshoppers. "In eating they give the preference to the former, being oily and the latter not."[6]

On the Pacific Coast, tribes had been dealing with white men for years. In addition to trapping and trading furs, these "canoe Indians" usually had food to offer. Ross Cox described Indians drying salmon on the Columbia River: "About four or five miles above the fall, a high rocky island three miles in length lies in the center of the river, on which the Indians were employed drying salmon, great quantities of which were cured and piled under broad boards in stacks."[7]

What these Indians most wanted in trade were axes. For the work of cutting down trees and making canoes, Cox discovered, they had used only chisels and stones.

"With these wretched implements, and wedges made of hemlock knots steeped in oil and hardened by the fire," Gabriel Franchere noted, "they would undertake to cut down the largest cedars of the forest, to dig them out and fashion them into canoes, to split them and get out the boards wherewith to build their houses."[8]

The Native Americans were an invaluable source of information about the land ahead, and sometimes they could be persuaded to join the expeditions as guides and

*The Klamath Indians used dugout canoes to gather reeds for mats
and baskets.*

interpreters. During the worst of times, Indians saved trappers' lives.

"There was no game to be procured and our only resource was the flesh of horses which died of starvation and exposure to the storm," related mountain man Jim Beckwourth in 1824–1825. "It was midwinter, and every thing around us bore a gloomy aspect. We were without provisions, and we saw no means of obtaining any. At this crisis, six or seven Indians of the Pawnee Loup band came into our camp. . . . They invited us to their lodges. . . . The Indians . . . spread a feast. . . . Our horses, too, were well cared for, and soon assumed a more rotund appearance."[9]

Although friendly exchanges were common, hostility could develop without warning. Members of the Mojave people "in large numbers and with most perfect semblance of peace and friendship were aiding the party to cross the river," Jedediah Smith recounted of an incident on the Colorado River. As soon as the party was divided, with some on both sides of the river and some still on the rafts, the Mojave "suddenly rose upon them and surrounding the party in a most unexpected moment and manner" began to attack.[10] Nine of nineteen men were killed.

Being prepared for an attack and willing to fight was just part of the mountain life. James Clyman told of his first encounter, on the Ashley expedition in 1823. The Arikara, who lived on the Missouri River, feared they would lose trading power if the fur trappers moved upriver past them. They attacked the expedition, killed thirteen men and wounded ten or eleven.

"Before meeting with this defeat I think few men had Stronger Ideas of their bravery and disregard of fear than I had," Clyman recalled, "but standing on a bear and open sand barr to be shot at from behind a picketed Indian village was more than I had contacted for and some what cooled my courage."[11]

Sometimes violence grew out of the tension of trading or outright theft. A party with Jedediah Smith and the clerk Harrison Rogers had been "trading shell and scale fish, rasberrys, strawberrys . . . also some fur skins" with Native Americans near the Oregon coast. Then the atmosphere changed. One Indian "got mad on account of a trade he made and killed the mules and horses." Another Indian stole an ax, "and we were obliged to seize him for the purpose of tying him before we could scare him to make him give it up."[12]

Two days later, the whole company—except for two—were murdered before breakfast. Because Smith and another man had left the camp early to scout the route for the day, they survived and eventually recovered the journal kept by Rogers.

Such massacres incensed the incoming Americans, but the Indians, too, had good reasons for anger. The massacred clerk had observed the harsh treatment Indians received in the California missions. His party had been quite hospitably received by the prosperous San Gabriel Arcángel mission, where most of the work was done by more than 1,000 Indian men, women, and children.

They "are kept in great fear"; Rogers recorded. "For the least offense they are corrected; they are compleat slaves in every sense of the word." On Sunday, "There was five Inds. brought to the mission by two other Inds, who act as constables, or overseers, and sentenced to be whiped for not going to work when ordered.

"Each received from 12 to 14 lashes on their bare posteriors; they were all old men, say from 50 to 60 years of age, the commandant standing by with his sword to see that the Ind. who flogged them done his duty."[13]

Catherine, too, witnessed violence on the expedition with her father in 1841. After camping by a village of Indians, the trappers found that four or five of their traps had been stolen, and they were enraged.

"At last the trappers resolved to make a day of revenge for their five traps and designed to attack the Indians in their own camp unawares. My father was invited to join in the bloody work, but he refused saying, 'I did not come here to war but to catch fur. These Indians may know nothing about your traps. They may have been taken by some distant thieves. Why arm to murder these poor hospitable people? They have no arms but clubs and bows. Why do you take rifles? . . . Take clubs only, if you are brave men but I will not be with you.'"[14]

The next morning the trappers attacked the village, killing all the men, women, and children or forcing them into the river where they drowned.

Attacks on fur trappers did not stop the fur trade, and killing whole villages did not end the Indian theft or attacks. Rather, the Indians were further weakened by warfare with each other, by loss of trade, by the near extinction of the buffalo, and by disease.

"This evening a conversation was had upon the subject of the diminution of the buffaloe," William Anderson wrote in 1834, "which several of the oldest mountaineers pronounced to be very considerable." Just three years before, the conversation revealed, the Sioux had traded 50,000 buffalo robes. "For this trade, it is to be remembered the cows only are killed—From this an idea, of the

Buffalo were nearly wiped out by white hunters in the late 1880s. Thanks to conservation efforts, buffalo herds are increasing. They roam in U.S. national parks and on fenced game preserves. About 15,000 buffalo also roam in Canada.

immense numbers of these animals which are yearly destroyed, may be formed."[15]

The Indians' biggest enemy was the disease brought by the newcomers. By the 1830s, smallpox had come up the Missouri River on an American Fur Company steamboat. Just two years after the Blackfeet harassed his fall trapping party, Kit Carson wrote that they were no longer a problem. The Crows told them smallpox was among the Blackfeet and they had gone north of the Missouri. In 1837 the disease swept across the prairies and into the mountains, wiping out the friendly Mandans and about two-thirds of the Blackfeet.

In the contact between native peoples and newcomers, some of the racial lines began to blur. "An Indian belonging to a small tribe on the coast to the southward of the Clatsops, occasionally visited the fort," at Astoria, Ross Cox noted. "His history was rather curious. His skin was fair, his face partially freckled, and his hair quite red. . . . The Indians allege that his father was an English sailor who had deserted from a sailing vessel, and had lived many years among their tribe, one of whom he married."[16]

The so-called half-breed sons and daughters of these couples were often wise in both cultures. When she grew up, Catherine married Angus McDonald, a Scottish employee of the Hudson's Bay Company. To her children she told of traveling with her father, always on the watch, "my eyes being young and strong."[17] McDonald copied the stories into a ledger as she told them, thus preserving a rare Native American account of the fur-trapping life.

GUIDES FOR
THE EMIGRANTS

Beaver was getting scarce," Kit Carson wrote of the year 1841, "and, finding it was necessary to try our hand at something else," he found a new job. Carson became a hunter for Bent's Fort on the Arkansas River in Colorado. He was paid a dollar a day.[1]

Jedediah Smith, too, left the mountain life. Advising a young man from Connecticut against going into the Rockies, Smith told him "the chances were much greater in favor of meeting death than of finding restoration to health. . . " According to the young man, "[Smith] said that he had spent above eight years in the mountains and should not return to them."[2]

Besides the depletion of the beaver and the dangers of mountain life, the mountain men also foresaw the coming of settlers. "No doubt ere many years a colony will be formed on this stream," wrote fur trapper Peter Skene Ogden at the site of Portland, Oregon, "and I am of the opinion it will with little care flourish."[3]

Before settlements could flourish, however, the settlers had to get there. It was the mountain men who knew which rivers were navigable, which ridges were passes through the mountains, and which Indians were friendly. Many of the trappers became guides for everyone else who wanted to come west.

Returning to St. Louis from his work as a hunter in the spring of 1842, Kit Carson discovered that a guide was needed for an expedition led by Colonel John C. Frémont. Frémont made several expeditions across the West for the U.S. government. The purpose of this trip was to choose sites for military posts along the Oregon Trail, the trail that would be used by the emigrants. "I spoke to Colonel Fremont, informed him that I had been some time in the mountains and thought I could guide him to any point he would wish to go," Carson wrote.[4] He was offered and accepted $100 a month as a guide and hunter.

Two years later, James Clyman joined a group of about 500 people traveling west in 100 wagons. He had been farming in Illinois but decided to roam again. He enjoyed the new mix of people traveling west.

"[May] 23 a fine clear night and a pleasant morning walked out through camp observed all sizes and ages Several fine intelegent young Ladies engaged one of them to make me a pair of Pantaloons."[5]

The emigrants also brought with them small comforts, which Clyman had never known in the mountains: "At our usual hour of camping we came to a small Brook whare a company of them ware Just coming up to camp Likewise and they came to us with Pail fulls of good new milk which to us was a treat of greate rarity after so many long tiresome days travel."[6]

John Charles Frémont

Passing close to a place where he had camped before, Clyman noted that the "mountains look quite familiar allthough I have not seen them for 17 years and it appears as if the 17 summers last past had not in the least diminished the snow that then crownd their lofty heads which still ware the white appearance of old age."[7]

His caravan arrived in Willamette Falls, Oregon, in October 1844, with no great calamities. Roving east again two years later, Clyman encountered even more people heading west: "When we came in sight of N. Platte we had the Pleasant sight of Beholding the valy to a greate distance dotted with Peopl Horses cattle wagons and Tents their being 30 wagons all Buisily engaged in crossing the River."[8]

He wondered about their reasons for moving: "It is remarkable how anxious thes people are to hear from the Pacific country and strange that so many of all kinds and classes of People should sell out comfortable homes in Missouri and elsewhare pack up and start across such an emmence Barren waste to settle in some new Place of which they have at most so uncertain information, but this is the character of my countrymen."[9]

Clyman was tempted to warn them of the hardships they faced. "Today we met all most one continual stream of Emigrants ending their long and Tedious march to oregon & california and I found it allmost impossible to pass these honest looking open harted people without giving them some slight discription of what they might Expect in their newly adopted and anxious sought for new home."[10]

The next evening his party camped "with a company for california an they kept in conversation untill near midnight."[11] Clyman warned them against taking the route he had just come, the Hastings Cutoff, but they didn't take his advice. This was the famous Donner party that became stranded in the Sierra Nevada over the winter, some of them starving to death.

While some mountain men like Clyman became

A wagon train crossing a valley in the Rocky Mountains.

guides for the wagon trains and others like Carson were hunters or scouts for army expeditions, still others found new areas for trading. In 1831 Jedediah Smith entered the Sante Fe trade, taking textiles, cottons, silks, calicoes, velvets, and hardware from Missouri to trade for horses, mules, gold and silver bullion in New Mexico, which at that time was part of Mexico. Another former trapper, James Beckwourth, also spent ten years in the Southwest, trading along the Santa Fe Trail. One skill he used was finding Native Americans—the customers he wanted to trade with.

Jedediah S. Smith

Once in Cheyenne country he sent three different messengers out to find customers, and they all returned without success. "Tired of these failures, I took a man with me, and started in the direction of the Laramie mountain. While ascending the mount, I cast my eyes in the direction of a valley, and discovered buffalo running in small groups, which was sufficient evidence that they had been chased recently by Indians. We went no farther, but encamped there, and at nightfall we saw fires. The next morning a dense smoke hung like a cloud over the village of the Cheyennes; we ate a hasty meal, and started to pay them a visit."[12]

Other mountain men used their experience with Indians to fight them. After three men in Frémont's expedition were killed by Klamaths in 1846, Kit Carson was sent after them. Carson soon found a village and killed a number of the inhabitants, but he didn't stop there. "Their houses were built of flag, beautifully woven. They had been fishing [and] had in their houses some ten wagon loads of fish they had caught. All their fishing tackle, camp equipment, etc. was there," Carson noted without the regret John Boit had expressed more than fifty years earlier.

"I wished to do them as much damage as I could, so I directed their houses to be set on fire. The flag being dry it was a beautiful sight. The Indians had commenced the war with us without cause and I thought they should be chastized in a summary manner. And they were severely punished."[13]

James Clyman took a broader view. As more Americans from the eastern states moved across the country, confrontations with the Indian tribes were inevitable. Some authority was needed, he felt, to maintain peace between the two: "Heard that a small party of men started for the states about a month since ware stoped by the snake Indians on account of Two of That nation being killed by some Stragling americans that came through the latter part of the winter," he wrote in May 1845. "This circumstance shews the great necesity of some authority being Established along this rout it being allmost amatter of necessity that people should be able to pass and repass in measureable security from and to the states."[14] Eventually the army took over the job of separating the native people from the newcomers who wanted the land they inhabited.

Even with these conflicts, Jim Beckwourth thought the emigrants had life easier than did mountain men. "When I recurred to my own adventures, I would smile at the comparison of their sufferings with what myself and other men of the mountains had really endured in former times," he remembered as he settled down to life as a hotelkeeper and trader in a California valley.

"The forts that now afford protection to the traveler were built by ourselves at the constant peril of our lives, amid Indian tribes nearly double their present numbers. Without wives and children to comfort us on our lonely way; without well-furnished wagons to resort to when hungry, no roads before us but trails temporarily made; our clothing consisting of the skins of animals that had fallen before our unerring rifles, and often whole days on insufficient rations, or entirely without food; occasionally our whole party on guard the entire night, and our strength deserting us through unceasing watching and fatigue; these are sufferings that made theirs appear trivial, and ours surpass in magnitude my power of relation."[15]

Despite Beckwourth's assessment, the mountain men

and the emigrants shared the same spirit. Camped at a stream in July 1846, James Clyman found the grave of "Mrs Sarak Keys agead 70 yares who had departed this life in may last." The grave set him to wondering why a seventy-year-old woman would undertake "this long tedious and even dangerous Journy." He decided it was because "the human mind can never be satisfied never at rest allways on the strech for something new some strange novelty."[16] It was the reason they all—explorer, trapper, guide, and emigrant—kept on stretching west.

SOURCE NOTES

INTRODUCTION: FIRST GLIMPSES

1. Don De Nevi and Noel Francis Moholy, *Junípero Serra* (New York: Harper and Row, 1985), 39.

2. Gabriel Franchere, *Narrative of a Voyage to the Northwest Coast of America in the Years 1811, 1812, 1813 and 1814* (Chicago: R. R. Donnelly and Sons, 1954), 24.

3. Dale L. Morgan and Eleanor Towles Harris, eds., *The Rocky Mountain Journals of William Marshall Anderson* (San Marino: The Huntington Library, 1967), 69.

4. "Pages on the Past," *History in the Making,* Videorecording. Seattle, Wash.: Camera One, 1988. Gary Warriner, director/filmmaker.

5. Gene Olson and Joan Olson, *Washington Times and Trails* (Rogue River, Ore.: Windyridge Press, 1970), 2.

6. De Nevi and Moholy, *Junípero Serra*, 74.

7. Donald Cutter, *Malaspina and Galiano: Spanish Voyages to the Northwest Coast, 1791–92* (Seattle: University of Washington Press, 1991), 85.

8. Ibid.

9. Franchere, *Narrative of a Voyage to the Northwest Coast of America in the Years 1811, 1812, 1813 and 1814*, 21.

10. De Nevi and Moholy, *Junípero Serra*, 128.

11. Cutter, *Malaspina and Galiano: Spanish Voyages to the Northwest Coast, 1791–92*, 85.

12. William Wood, *Elizabethan Sea Dogs* (New York: U.S. Publishers Assoc., Yale University Press, 1918), 138.

13. Frank Alfred Golder, *Bering's Voyages: An Account of the Efforts of the Russians to Determine the Relation of Asia and America*, vol. 1. New York: American Geographical Society, 1922–25. July 20, 1741, entry.

14. Morgan and Harris, *The Rocky Mountain Journals of William Marshall Anderson*, 69

1. THE JOURNEY

1. F. W. Howay, ed., *Voyages of the Columbia to the Northwest Coast, 1787–1790 and 1790–1793* (Boston: The Massachusetts Historical Society, 1941), 363.

2. Franchere, *Narrative of a Voyage to the Northwest Coast of America in the Years 1811, 1812, 1813 and 1814*, 10.

3. Ibid., 13, 14.

4. Howay, *Voyages of the Columbia to the Northwest Coast, 1787–1790 and 1790–1793*, 367.

5. Ibid., 368.

6. Captain James Cook, *Voyages to the North Pacific Ocean* (London: Hakluyt Society, 1784), 1088.

7. Howay, *Voyages of the Columbia to the Northwest Coast, 1787–1790 and 1790–1793*, 369.

8. Franchere, *Narrative of a Voyage to the Northwest Coast of America in the Years 1811, 1812, 1813 and 1814*, 49.

9. Benito de la Sierra, *California Historical Society*

Quarterly "Fray Sierra Journal." 9 (Sept. 1930), March 31, 1775.

10. Desmond Wilcox, *Ten Who Dared* (Boston: Time-Life Television Book, Little Brown, 1977).

11. De la Sierra, "Fray Sierra Journal," May 11, 1775.

12. Ibid., July 23, 1775.

13. Ibid., August 11, 1775.

14. Ibid., August 31, 1775.

15. Howay, *Voyages of the Columbia to the Northwest Coast, 1787–1790 and 1790–1793*, 369.

16. De la Sierra, "Fray Sierra Journal," June 4, 1775.

17. Ibid., July 10, 1775.

18. Ibid., July 12, 1775.

19. Cutter, *Malaspina and Galiano: Spanish Voyages to the Northwest Coast, 1791–92*, 70.

20. Franchere, *Narrative of a Voyage to the Northwest Coast of America in the Years 1811, 1812, 1813 and 1814*, 281.

21. De la Sierra, "Fray Sierra Journal," November 20, 1775.

2. ENCOUNTERS ALONG THE COAST

1. Cutter, *Malaspina and Galiano: Spanish Voyages to the Northwest Coast, 1791–92*, 26.

2. Harrison Clifford Dale, *The Explorations of William H. Ashley and Jedediah Smith, 1822–29* (Lincoln: University of Nebraska Press, 1991), 263.

3. Franchere, *Narrative of a Voyage to the Northwest Coast of America in the Years 1811, 1812, 1813 and 1814*, 108.

4. F. W. Hodge and T. H. Lewis, eds., *Spanish Explorers in the Southern United States* (New York: C. Scribner's Sons, 1907), 307.

5. Howay, *Voyages of the Columbia to the Northwest Coast, 1787–1790 and 1790–1793*, 383.

6. Ibid., 369.

7. Cook, *Voyages to the North Pacific Ocean*, 1089.

8. Golder, *Bering's Voyages*, 273.

9. Hodge and Lewis, *Spanish Explorers in the Southern United States*, 311–312.

10. Howay, *Voyages of the Columbia to the Northwest Coast, 1787–1790 and 1790–1793*, 372.

11. Hodge and Lewis, *Spanish Explorers in the Southern United States*, 350.

12. De Nevi and Moholy, *Junipero Serra*, 85.

13. Cutter, *Malaspina and Galiano: Spanish Voyages to the Northwest Coast, 1791–92*, 32.

14. Cook, *Voyages to the North Pacific Ocean*, 1089.

15. Howay, *Voyages of the Columbia to the Northwest Coast, 1787–1790 and 1790–1793*

16. Ibid., 370, 374.

17. Ibid., 399.

18. Cutter, *Malaspina and Galiano: Spanish Voyages to the Northwest Coast, 1791–92*, 116.

19. Ibid., 76.

20. Howay, *Voyages of the Columbia to the Northwest Coast, 1787–1790 and 1790–1793*, 390–391.

21. Ibid.

22. Cutter, *Malaspina and Galiano: Spanish Voyages to the Northwest Coast, 1791–92*, 373.

3. EXPLORING THE INTERIOR

1. Roy Daniels, *Alexander Mackenzie and the Northwest* (New York: Barnes and Noble, 1969), 149.

2. Bernard DeVoto, ed., *The Journals of Lewis and Clark* (Boston: Houghton Mifflin, 1953), 294.

3. John Bakeless, *The Journals of Lewis and Clark* (New York: Penguin Books), 1964.

4. Patrick Gass, *Sgt. Gass's Journal of the Lewis and Clark Expedition* (Chicago: A. C. McClurg and Co., 1904), 2.

5. Ibid., 37, 20, 86–87, 29.

6. Charles Preuss, *Exploring with Fremont* (Norman, Okla.: University of Oklahoma Press, 1958), 49.

7. Gass, *Sgt. Gass's Journal of the Lewis and Clark Expedition*, 145.

8. DeVoto, *The Journals of Lewis and Clark*, 294.

9. Gass, *Sgt. Gass's Journal of the Lewis and Clark Expedition*, 187–188.

10. Alexander Mackenzie, *Voyages from Montreal Through the Continent of North America to the Frozen and Pacific Oceans in 1789 and 1793, with an Account of the Rise and State of the Fur Trade* (Rutland, Vt.: Charles E. Tuttle, 1971), 24.

11. James P. Ronda, *Astoria and Empire* (Lincoln and London: University of Nebraska Press, 1990), 24.

12. Preuss, *Exploring with Fremont*, 92.

13. Ronda, *Astoria and Empire*, 194.

14. Franchere, *Narrative of a Voyage to the Northwest Coast of America in the Years 1811, 1812, 1813 and 1814*, 143.

15. Ibid., 163.

16. Ross Cox, *Adventures on the Columbia River* (Portland, Ore.: Binford and Mort, 1957), 15.

17. Ibid., 17.

18. Ibid.

19. John Davies, *Douglas of the Forests: The North American Journals of David Douglas* (Seattle: University of Washington Press, 1980), 39.

20. Ibid., 42–43.

21. Ibid., 103.

22. Ibid., 76.

23. Franchere, *Narrative of a Voyage to the Northwest Coast of America in the Years 1811, 1812, 1813 and 1814*, 281.

24. Cox, *Adventures on the Columbia River*, 97.

4. THE FUR-TRAPPING LIFE

1. Dale, *The Explorations of William H. Ashley and Jedediah Smith, 1822–29*, 64.

2. James Clyman, *Journal of a Mountain Man* (Missoula, Mont.: Mountain Press, 1984), 9.

3. Ibid.

4. Morgan and Harris, *The Rocky Mountain Journals of William Marshall Anderson*, 32.

5. Winona Adams, ed., "An Indian Girl's Story of a Trading Expedition to the Southwest about 1841," *Montana University Historical Reprints Series*, no. 11 (Missoula, Mont.: State University of Montana), 3.

6. Dale, *The Explorations of William H. Ashley and Jedediah Smith, 1822–29*, 268.

7. Morgan and Harris, *The Rocky Mountain Journals of William Marshall Anderson*, 128.

8. Ibid., 125.

9. Preuss, *Exploring with Fremont*, 24.

10. Dale, *The Explorations of William H. Ashley and Jedediah Smith, 1822–29*, 190.

11. Clyman, *Journal of a Mountain Man*, 241.

12. Harvey L. Carter, *Dear Old Kit* (Norman, Okla.: University of Oklahoma Press, 1968), 81.

13. Preuss, *Exploring with Fremont*, 108.

14. Clyman, *Journal of a Mountain Man*, 187.

15. Ibid., 198.

16. Morgan and Harris, *The Rocky Mountain Journals of William Marshall Anderson*, 169.

17. Adams, "An Indian Girl's Story of a Trading Expedition to the Southwest about 1841," 14.

18. Morgan and Harris, *The Rocky Mountain Journals of William Marshall Anderson*, 141.

19. Ibid., 141.

20. Carter, *Dear Old Kit*, 61.

21. Morgan and Harris, *The Rocky Mountain Journals of William Marshall Anderson*, 189.

5. CONTACT AND CONFLICT

1. Gass, *Sgt. Gass's Journal of the Lewis and Clark Expedition*, 41.

2. Ibid., 235.

3. Ibid., 92.

4. Carter, *Dear Old Kit*, 61.

5. Patrick Gass, 128.

6. Archie Binns, *Peter Skene Ogden: Fur Trader* (Portland, Ore.: Binford and Mort, 1967), 168.

7. Cox, 15.

8. Franchere, *Narrative of a Voyage to the Northwest Coast of America in the Years 1811, 1812, 1813 and 1814*, 189.

9. Elinor Wilson, *Jim Beckwourth: Black Mountain Man and War Chief of the Crows* (Norman, Okla.: University of Oklahoma Press, 1972), 35.

10. Dale, *The Explorations of William H. Ashley and Jedediah Smith, 1822–29*, 228.

11. Clyman, *Journal of a Mountain Man*, 15.

12. Dale, *The Explorations of William H. Ashley and Jedediah Smith, 1822–29*, 272, 275.

13. Ibid., 204.

14. Adams, "An Indian Girl's Story of a Trading Expedition to the Southwest about 1841," 12.

15. Morgan and Harris, *The Rocky Mountain Journals of William Marshall Anderson*, 178.

16. Cox, *Adventures on the Columbia River*, 56–57.

17. Adams, "An Indian Girl's Story of a Trading Expedition to the Southwest about 1841," 5.

6. GUIDES FOR THE EMIGRANTS

1. Carter, *Dear Old Kit*, 71.

2. Dale, *The Explorations of William H. Ashley and Jedediah Smith, 1822–29*, 299.

3. Binns, *Peter Skene Ogden*, 84.

4. Carter, *Dear Old Kit*, 81.

5. Clyman, *Journal of a Mountain Man*, 73.

6. Ibid., 260.

7. Ibid., 109.

8. Ibid., 260.

9. Ibid.

10. Ibid.

11. Ibid., 261.

12. Wilson, *Jim Beckwourth: Black Mountain Man and War Chief of the Crows*, 99.

13. Carter, *Dear Old Kit*, 105.

14. Clyman, *Journal of a Mountain Man*, 173.

15. Wilson, *Jim Beckwourth: Black Mountain Man and War Chief of the Crows*, 39.

16. Clyman, *Journal of a Mountain Man*, 265.

FURTHER READING

BOOKS

Aaseng, Nathan. *From Rags to Riches*. Minneapolis: Lerner, 1990.

Alter, Judith. *Growing Up in the Old West*. Chicago: Watts, 1991.

———. *Women of the Old West*. New York: Watts, 1989.

Bakeless, John, ed. *The Journals of Lewis and Clark*. New York: Penguin, 1964.

Bennett, Robert Allen. *We'll All Go Home in the Spring*. Walla Walla, Wash.: Pioneer Press, 1984.

Binns, Archie. *Peter Skene Ogden: Fur Trader*. Portland, Ore.: Binford and Mort, 1967.

Blumberg, Rhoda. *The Great American Gold Rush*. New York: Macmillan, 1989.

Brown, Dee. *Gentle Tamers: Women in the Old Wild West*. Lincoln: University of Nebraska Press, 1968.

———. *Hear That Lonesome Whistle Blow: Railroads in the West*. New York: Holt, 1977.

Carter, Harvey L. *Dear Old Kit*. Norman: University of Oklahoma Press, 1968.

Clappe, Louise (Dame Shirley). *The Shirley Letters: From the*

California Mines, 1850–1852. Edited by Carl I. Wheat. New York: Knopf, 1961.

Clemens, Samuel Langhorne. *Roughing It.* New York: Holt, Rinehart and Winston, 1965.

De Nevi, Don, and Noel Moholy. *Junípero Serra.* New York: Harper and Row, 1985.

Erickson, Paul. *Daily Life in a Covered Wagon.* Washington, D.C.: Preservation Press, 1994.

Fischer, Christiane, ed. *Let Them Speak for Themselves: Women in the American West, 1849–1900.* Hamden, Conn.: Archon, 1977.

Fisher, Leonard Everett. *The Oregon Trail.* New York: Holiday, 1990.

Harte, Bret. *The Luck of Roaring Camp.* Providence, Rhode Island: Jamestown, 1976.

Hoobler, Dorothy, and Thomas Hoobler. *Treasure in the Stream: The Story of a Gold Rush Girl.* Morristown, New Jersey: Silver Burdett, 1991.

Jessett, Thomas E. *Chief Spokan Garry.* Minneapolis: T. S. Denison, 1960.

Johnson, Paul C., ed. *The California Missions.* Menlo Park, Cal.: Lane Book, 1964.

Katz, William. *The Black West.* Seattle: Open Hand, 1987.

Lapp, Rudolph. *Blacks in Gold Rush California.* New Haven: Yale University Press, 1977.

Lasky, Kathryn. *Beyond the Divide.* New York: Dell, 1986.

Levy, Jo Ann. *They Saw the Elephant.* Hamden, Conn.: Archon, 1990.

Lewis, Oscar. *Sutter's Fort: Gateway to the Gold Fields.* New York: Knopf, 1976.

Luchetti, Cathy, and Carol Olwell. *Women of the West.* Berkeley: Antelope Island Press, 1982.

McNeer, May. *The California Gold Rush.* New York: Random House, 1987.

Meltzer, Milton. *The Chinese Americans: A History in Their Own Words.* New York: HarperCollins, 1980.

Morris, Juddi. *The Harvey Girls: The Women Who Civilized the West.* New York: Walker, 1994.

Moynihan, Ruth B., Susan Armitage, and Christiane Fischer Duchamp, eds. *So Much to Be Done: Women Settlers on the Mining and Ranching Frontier.* Lincoln: University of Nebraska Press, 1990.

Nabakov, Peter. *Native American Testimony: An Anthology of Indian and White Relations, First Encounter to Dispossession.* New York: HarperCollins, 1972.

Rappaport, Doreen, ed. *American Women: Their Lives in Their Words.* New York: HarperCollins, 1992.

Ray, Delia. *Gold, the Klondike Adventure.* New York: Lodestar, 1989.

Schlissel, Lillian. *Women's Diaries of the Westward Journey.* New York: Shocken, 1982.

Smith, Carter. *Bridging the Continent: A Sourcebook on the American West.* Brookfield, Conn.: Millbrook Press, 1992.

Steber, Rick. *Grandpa's Stories.* Prineville, Ore.: Bonanza, 1991.

Stewart, George R. *The Pioneers Go West.* New York: Random House, 1987.

Stratton, Joanna. *Pioneer Women.* New York: Simon and Schuster, 1982.

The Trailblazers. *The Old West.* New York: Time-Life Books, 1979.

Tunis, Edwin. *Frontier Living.* New York: HarperCollins, 1976.

Van Steenwyk, Elizabeth. *The California Gold Rush: West with the Forty-niners.* Chicago: Watts, 1991.

Watt, James W. *Journal of Mule Train Packing in Eastern Washington in the 1860s.* Fairfield, Wash.: Ye Galleon Press, 1978.

Weis, Norman D. *Helldorados, Ghosts and Camps of the Old Southwest.* Caldwell, Idaho: Caxton Printers, 1977.

Wilder, Laura Ingalls. *West from Home*. New York: HarperCollins, 1974.

Wilson, Elinor. *Jim Beckwourth: Black Mountain Man and War Chief of the Crows*. Norman: University of Oklahoma Press, 1972.

Young, Alida O. *Land of the Iron Dragon*. New York: Doubleday, 1978.

TAPES AND COMPUTER SOFTWARE

American West: Myth and Reality, Clear View, CD-ROM.

Dare, Bluff, or Die, Software Tool Works, CD-ROM, DOS.

Miner's Cave, MECC, Apple II.

Morrow, Honere. *On to Oregon!* Recorded Books, Inc., Prince Frederick, Md. Three cassettes.

Murphy's Minerals, MECC, Apple II.

Oregon Trail II, CD-ROM, Windows.

The Oregon Trail, MECC, Apple II, MS-DOS, 1990.

Santa Fe Trail (Educational Activities).

Steber, Rick. *Grandpa's Stories*. Bonanza. Cassette.

Wagons West, Focus Media, 485 South Broadway, Suite 12, Hicksville, New York, 11801.

INDEX

Alaska, 24, 26, 28
Anderson, William Marshall,
    11, 14, 17, 60, 61
army as regional authority, 80
Astoria expedition, 42–50
Astor, John Jacob, 41

Beckwourth, Jim, 68, 78, 80
Bering Strait, 17, 31
Blackfeet Indians, 65, 71
Boit, John, 19, 21, 22, 30,31, 34, 35
buffalo, 63, 65, 70, 79

California, 11, 24, 27, 35
Carson, Kit, 58, 60, 61, 65, 71,
    73, 74, 79
Cheyenne Indians, 79
Clark, William, 37–42
clothing, 31–33
Clyman, James, 51–52, 58,
    68–69, 74–76, 79, 81

Columbia, 21, 22, 23, 25, 30, 34
Columbia River, 15, 22, 40, 41,
    44, 45, 47, 66
Continental Divide, 55
Cook, Captain James, 22, 25,
    30, 33, 34
Coronado, Francisco Vásquez
    de, 19, 20, 29, 31, 64
Cox, Ross, 45–46, 48, 50, 66, 72
Crow Indians, 55, 71

Discovery, 22
Donner party, 76
Douglas, David, 47–49
Drake, Francis, 13, 15

Estevanico, 13, 19
explorers
    coastal expeditions, 63
    cultural differences with
        natives, 28–29, 31

first encounters with
natives, 28–36
graffiti as claim to land, 37
hardships, 13, 20-21, 55, 57
leaving their mark, 15–17,
24, 27, 37
naming places, 22, 28
overland expeditions, 63

Far West, 11, 17, 19, 46, 48, 62
food, 34, 39, 46, 58–59, 60,
65–66, 68
food aboard ships, 21–22
Franchere, Gabriel, 11, 14,
20–21, 27, 45, 48, 50, 66
Frémont, John C., 57, 74, 75, 79
Fuca, Juan de, 13, 27, 36
fur trading, 29, 33, 34, 35, 37,
41, 42, 50

Gass, Patrick, 38–40, 64, 65
Gray, Robert Captain, 19, 22,
23, 30, 35,
Great Salt Lake, 55–56
guides, 66, 68, 73–81
guiding emigrants, 73– 81
guiding wagon trains, 78
Indians as, 66, 68
scouts for army expeditions,
78

Hezeta, Bruno de, 24, 25, 27
Hudson's Bay Company, 47,
48, 72
Hunt, Wilson Price, 43– 44

Lewis and Clark expedition,
37–42, 43, 63, 65
Lewis, Meriwether, 37–42

Mackenzie, Alexander, 37, 41
Malaspina, Alejandro, 14, 26
Malaspina expedition, 26
Missouri River, 38, 39, 43, 51,
52, 63, 65, 68, 71
Mohave Indians, 68

Northwest coast, 30, 35
North West Company, 50

Ogden, Peter Skene, 65–66,
73
Oregon Trail, 46

Pacific Coast, 40, 63, 66
Pacific Northwest, 28
Pacific Ocean, 11, 13
pictographs, 15, 16
Plains Indians, 64–65
Puget Sound, 15, 27

reasons for exploring
bring Christianity to New
World, 14
find waterways, 38
look for water passage to
Orient, 13
political, 14
scientific, 14, 47–49
search for gold and silver,
27, 31
see strange lands, 14

Rio Grande, 13
Rocky Mountains, 38, 39, 46,
    51, 55–56, 73, 77

Samwell, David, 22
Sandwich Islands, 22
scurvy, 24–26, 27
sea, conditions on, 25– 27
sea otters, 50, 52, 61
Serra, Junípero, 11, 12,14, 19, 33
settlers, 74
settlers' hardships, 80
ships' supplies, 24–25
Sierra, Benito de la, 24,25, 27
Sioux Indians, 38, 43, 63–65, 70
smallpox, 36, 71
Smith, Jedediah, 55, 57, 68, 69,
    73, 78
Southwest, 28, 29, 78
Spain, 13, 14, 15, 19, 31
Spanish Tonquin, 21
Suria, Tomas de, 26, 36
Swi-net-klas, 28

Thompson, David, 41
traders, 19, 22, 27, 28–36, 45
trading, 29, 33–34, 35, 46, 66, 78

trappers, 29, 51–62, 65–71
    attack Indian village, 70
    beaver, 50, 51, 73
    becoming guides, 62, 74
    bring smallpox to Indians,
        71
    clothing, 52
    completed central overland
        route to Pacific, 57
    families, 54
    food, 65–66, 68
    furs, 68, 70
    hardships, 58–59, 65–66, 68
    helped by Indians, 55
    methods of trapping, 52–53
    muskrat, 53
    obstacles faced, 54
    over-trapping, 50, 61, 73
    "possible sacks," 52
    violence between trappers
        and Indians, 69–70
    wiping out buffalo
        population, 70, 71

voyageurs, 41

water scarcity, 57–58